Burn

Book

This Book Belongs to:

Thanks for your purchase!
We hope you enjoy this Journal.
If you consider this notebook
useful please leave a review.

Thanks for your support.
You are Awesome!